Confident Parenting

It's Not Rocket Science

Becky Crowe

AuthorHouse™
1663 Liberty Drive
Bloomington, IN 47403
www.authorhouse.com
Phone: 1 (800) 839-8640

Published by AuthorHouse 04/26/2018

ISBN: 978-1-5462-3877-5 (sc)
ISBN: 978-1-5462-3878-2 (e)

Print information available on the last page.

Cover Illustration credits to Audrey Crowe

This book is printed on acid-free paper.

author**HOUSE**®

becky crowe

confident parenting

(it's not rocket science)

Confident Parenting
(It's Not Rocket Science)

By: Becky Crowe

To my husband John: for all of your love and support through my career changes and the bills that come with them. Special thanks for doing all of the cooking and supplying the recipes!

To my family (both sides): for providing so many children with ample opportunities from which to build, but by no means perfect, my parenting skills.

To my beautiful girls: for your ideas which added so much to this book and for your support as I hesitated to publish. Special thanks to Audrey for the cover design and Jeanine Boutiere (a.k.a. 'Ms.B' the art teacher) for helping her.

To Patrick Blackburn, my editor (and Michelle Evard Moses for recommending him!) Patrick you have no idea how much I appreciate your candor and support. I truly appreciate how patient you were with me!

Table of contents

Preface

Writing this book was a family effort. I would write sections as we drove to and from vacation and we would talk about what was going into it. John, Catherine and Audrey all had a say in what I should write about and added many anecdotes. They were my initial editors! Without them, I would have no grounds for writing this. Without them, I would not be the person I am today.

At the end of each chapter you will find a recipe. These are some of our favorite recipes and I thought that you might enjoy trying them with your family.

Chapter 1
It Really Isn't Rocket Science

"Nobody can make you feel inferior without your consent." ~**Eleanor Roosevelt**

For the most part, this book is common sense. But what I've learned over the years is that not everybody comes equipped with the common sense parenting gene. Many times I have heard parents state that they wish their kids came with instructions -- especially for the teenage years. This book may be the closest thing you get to a set of instructions for raising your children.

You may or may not agree with what I have to say or how we have chosen to raise our kids. How you do it is up to you. You can choose to follow in our footsteps or you can choose to go your own way. In fact, you will probably do a little bit of my way and a little bit of your own way. That's how parenting is: trial and error, use what you liked about how your parents raised you and discard what you disliked. So you'll do the same with this book. It's O.K. You'll develop your own parenting style in no time.

Right now you need to make a decision. Think about your philosophy in regards to raising children. If your philosophy involves raising children to live off the system or perhaps plan to have an au pair raise your children please go to Chapter 35.

If your philosophy involves raising your children to be ethical, responsible, independent, and productive members of society, please continue to chapter 2. Keep in mind that this book is not based on clinical studies but on my own personal experiences. I have read many child psychology articles and could cite them in this book but I choose to only cite what I feel strongly about. Why? Because how we have chosen to raise our children is not based on research or what Dr. Spock or anyone else said was the right thing to do. Just like most educated people, we have received information from books and people but it is experience that is the best teacher. You will learn from books you read AND from your own experiences, too.

As a guidance counselor, and even before, I have witnessed children, teens, and even adults who seem to be completely devoid of manners, respect and the whole idea of responsibility. A few things to note: 1. It is common courtesy to politely smile at people when passing them…even if you don't know them. 2. As a member of society, you have the responsibility to keep your world clean both figuratively and literally. Watch how you treat yourself and others and the world around you. Present yourself well and keep your world clean. OK… I'll get off of my soapbox and let you get to the rest of the book.

Shrimp and Asparagus Pasta

1. 1 bag frozen shrimp – med sized, raw, thawed
2. Old Bay seasoning to taste
3. 1TBP olive oil
4. 1 TBP butter
5. Hot pepper flakes
6. 1 lb. Penne pasta
7. 1 lb. asparagus
8. dash cayenne pepper

Cook pasta according to directions on box. Trim stems from asparagus and cut into pieces that are about the same size as the penne. Cook asparagus in salted water until easily pierced with knife. Drain. Set aside. Melt butter and oil in sauté pan. Add pepper flakes. Season shrimp with Old Bay and cayenne pepper and sauté with butter and oil until cooked (about 3-4 minutes). Toss in cooked pasta and asparagus. Stir to combine. Top with fresh grated cheese, such as Romano or Parmesan.

Chapter 2
The early years

"There are only two lasting bequests we can hope to give our children. One of these is roots; the other, wings."
~Hodding Carter

So this is how it went for my husband and me:

1993 - Got married

1995 – Madelaine, our first daughter, was stillborn the day before my cousin gave birth to her second child

1996 - Catherine was born less than one week after John's grandmother passed

Three months later I miscarried

1998 - Audrey was born two days after John's other grandmother passed

By the time we successfully birthed Audrey, I was done! Mentally, I couldn't take any more. Poor John had diarrhea the entire time I was pregnant – every time! So he was pretty much done too. You may be wondering why I am telling you this. The reason is simple. Nothing ever goes according to plan. For crying out loud does anyone actually plan to have a stillborn child? Of course not. So the point is, do what is right for you. Whether "you" are a single parent or a couple, do it your way. Don't let anyone else talk you into having more children than you want and certainly don't let your parents/friends tell you how to parent or allow them to make you feel guilty for the way you choose to parent.

So... after all of that, we focused on raising our two girls the best we could. We gave them what we could but also tried to teach them to be gracious, respectful and appreciative. I won't say we tried not to spoil them because, honestly, there was no chance of that. Our goal was to provide these girls with a better life than we had growing up. Don't get me wrong. John and I both had wonderful childhoods and our parents always met all of our basic needs and many of our '"wants". It's just a different world now. With the internet, the world is a much smaller place than it used to be. We wanted to make sure our kids knew what was out there. We wanted them to know that life is an adventure. We know way too many people who never leave their home town, are closed minded and think that people who don't speak English or are in any way different from themselves are bad. The reality is that we are all very similar. You just have to get out there and get to know other people and cultures.

We tried to create as many experiences as we could for them to learn from. They went to preschool so they could learn to socialize with their peers. It was a great start to learning how to meet and interact with new people. They had friends in our neighborhood but we felt it was important to expose them to other people. The sooner they learned to step outside of their comfort zone, the better off they would be in life.

We also made sure to set boundaries. It starts out simply with "no, you cannot have ice cream before you eat dinner", and moves to larger scale items such as a curfew for using their cell phone, a curfew when they go out with friends, or even how much money you are willing to spend on the clothes that they need and if they WANT more, they will have to spend their own money. Kids thrive when they are given boundaries; any parenting consultant will tell you that. It is up to you, the parent, to figure out what the rules and boundaries are and how you are going to handle them with your family. They NEED the boundaries and they NEED to know your expectations of them.

So the moral of this story is: Give them the world as you define it. Seriously. If you allow them to see what life is like for others, they will quickly appreciate what they have. If you provide them with rules, consequences for breaking those rules, and expectations of behavior, your children will thrive. Consequently, you will do your children a HUGE injustice if you choose to not follow through on this.

Fudge Pie

2oz semi-sweet chocolate

1c sugar

½ c butter

¼ c flour

2 eggs, beaten

1 tsp vanilla

1/8 tsp salt

Melt chocolate with butter in medium saucepan. Add beaten eggs then remaining ingredients. Mix well. Pour into greased   9inch pie plate. Bake at 325 for 30 minutes. Serve with a scoop of vanilla ice cream.

Chapter 3
The Practice Child

"While we try to teach our children all about life, our children teach us what life is all about."
~Angela Schwindt

I'll admit it -- we have made a lot of mistakes. Before you enter into parenthood, accept the fact that you are going to make mistakes too. There is no such thing as the perfect parent. Even within the same family, parents will differ in style. But those same parents will certainly have one thing in common: they will both make mistakes.

When Catherine was in 3rd grade, one day she was upset over something and started spouting off about how Audrey was allowed to do things and she wasn't. Their birthdays are close together and they had both gotten a Razor scooter from us. The conversation went something like this:

"MOM! Why does Audrey get a scooter? I had to wait until now. She should have to wait until she's eight, too."

I replied, "Sorry. We decided she could handle one."

"But she always gets to do things before I do!"

"Well," I said smiling, "that's because you're our practice child. We make all of our mistakes with you and then we know what we're doing for your sister."

While she wasn't totally satisfied with my answer, she caught the sarcasm and was able to laugh at the situation herself. Sometimes yelling back at them or getting upset with them for throwing a tantrum doesn't work. If you can keep a sense of humor about you, sometimes witty little comebacks work.

Just to let you know that you aren't the only one making mistakes, here are a few of the mistakes we have made. As you tell your stories to other parents, you'll find that they have made similar mistakes. The key is to learn from them. Don't repeat them. Then learn to laugh at them later.

Mistake 1

Catherine was about six months old. I placed her on the changing table at about 2 a.m. and walked across the room to get a dry sleeper. As I turned around, she was in mid air and landed on the carpet smack on the top of her head. I watched it happen in slow motion. I was beside myself. How many times had I been warned by my mom to NEVER EVER walk away from a baby on a changing table? Luckily, she was fine. She cried and was very scared but not injured.

Moral: NEVER EVER walk away from your child when you set them on a changing table. You may not be as lucky as I was. To be honest, this scared the heck out of me. I don't think I will ever laugh about this mistake.

Mistake 2

We were transplanting some houseplants in our backyard about a week after Catherine's first birthday. Suddenly she grabbed a handful of potting soil and stuffed it into her mouth! I tried to catch it and get it out but she had swallowed it before I could even reach her. We frantically called Poison Control, certain our little girl was in grave danger. Luckily, it wasn't a big deal and we just had to have her drink plenty of fluid and keep an eye on her. Several years later, we discovered the reason she thought she could eat the potting soil. Her birthday cake was Worms in Dirt which is Oreo cookie crumbs on top of chocolate pudding and gummy worms. Since we let her eat that…naturally she could have more of it when it is served in a big plastic bag!

Moral: Sometimes your children are going to get into things right under your nose. Be aware and be careful but don't beat yourself up over mistakes. Trust that you have done a great job childproofing your house in the best effort to keep your children safe. If they do get into something they shouldn't have, stay calm and seek help. And don't order a Worms in Dirt birthday cake!

Mistake 3

Catherine was about 1 ½ and we were giving her a bath. When she got out of the water, her little butt was bright red! John and I freaked out. We thought we had given her 3rd degree burns. We did what most first time parents would do and called John's mom. She told us that she had done the same thing and the redness would soon subside. As long as there aren't any blisters, she would be fine.

Moral: Use tepid water to bathe your children and ALWAYS test the water before they get in it!

Mistake 4

Catherine was 2 ½ and we had gone on vacation. During the vacation she complained a couple of times about her arm hurting and was always asking for chocolate milk. She loved drinking chocolate milk but it seemed like she was asking for it more often than usual. And she was not asking for water like she usually would. A week after we returned home, she was still drinking a lot of chocolate milk and occasionally complaining about her arm. We called the doctor and they had us do some general movement of her wrists and arm. She did them without complaining of pain so we disregarded the situation. A week later, she was still drinking the chocolate milk and periodically complaining about pain. We called the doctor again and decided to take her for x-rays. Low and behold… she had a broken arm. The doctor told us it looked like it had been almost healed. She needed to wear a cast for about a week. Imagine how we felt! Our child broke a bone and we had no idea. The best we can figure is that she had fallen when playing in the water fountains at the Tampa Zoo. But she didn't complain until later in the day.

Moral: Stuff happens! You cannot possibly prevent them from getting hurt or avoid making mistakes.

Over the years, we have made many more mistakes. The things we learned with Catherine weren't all negative. We learned that we too, are resilient. Having been through the loss of a child can leave one devastated. With the help of prayer, family, friends and the concepts in "When Bad Things Happen To Good People" (Kushner,

1981), we have succeeded. Catherine is beautiful inside and out. She is an independent thinker. As a matter of fact, in first grade she decided that she wanted people to call her by her initials. Now, everyone knows her as CC! She loves learning, traveling, and being creative. In school she participates in Model U.N and Mock Trial. She and her sister bring great joy to our life!

Our Shadow

From the very beginning Audrey was different from her sister. She stayed in the "oven" longer and she was a VBAC (vaginal birth after Caesarian). While some people would freak out over that, I stayed calm, remained positive and all went very smoothly.

This little girl's attitude is "anything you can do, she can do better". She loves roller coasters and all types of adventure and excitement. Catherine, on the other hand, has been to the hospital for stitches after falling into a table (age 1), broken arm (age 2), to remove a Polly Pocket toy from her nose (age 3), a wrist injury during gym class (age 12) and a roller skating ankle injury (age 13). Audrey has never been to the hospital outside of the day she was born. That's 12 years injury free! Amazing!

Audrey loves to fish and cook. She loves to work with her hands and learn new things. When she was four, we had new carpet installed in our house. Audrey put on her utility belt and helped the carpet layers. If our washer or dryer needed repair, Audrey was right there with the repairman. One of her favorite things to do is shadow John in the kitchen when he is making dinner. She also likes to help him with woodworking. She has an active imagination and enjoyed pretending that she was Supergirl by wrapping her animal blanket around her like a cape and rescuing us from pretend bad guys.

In Kindergarten, Audrey wore a Spiderman costume to school for Halloween. She is her own person, that's for sure! When she was nine, the secret of Santa was out of the bag. She didn't handle it as well as Catherine had done a few years earlier. One of my coworkers recommended a book called "Santa Are You for Real?" by Harold Myra. This was a Godsend! The book tells the story of the real St. Nicholas, who lived long ago. He secretly gave gifts to the children of the village. When he died, parents continued giving gifts to children in his honor. Even though Audrey still teases us for bursting her bubble years earlier, she has taken the story to heart. Every year, at Christmas, Audrey sneaks a little extra gift into everyone's stocking. It helped Audrey put the whole thing in perspective and it helped me through a very difficult parenting moment.

Audrey wants to grow up to be a roller coaster designer. Catherine wants to be a writer and U.S. Ambassador, or an Anthropologist. Each of your children will be unique and interesting in their own ways. Recognize it and cherish it!

Cookie Sundae

This is one of our favorite treats. It is made in one big skillet and served family style. We like to eat it out of the skillet together.

1 Tbsp butter

Frozen cookie dough

Vanilla ice cream

Caramel topping

Put a tablespoon of butter in a cast iron skillet. Place in oven to melt according to cookie package instructions. Place frozen cookie dough in skillet and cook according to package instructions. You will need enough cookies for the amount of people you are feeding. Once cooked, add a large scoop of ice cream on top. Drizzle with caramel and serve family style. Caution: Be careful not to touch the skillet when you are eating. It's hot!

Chapter 4
What Others Think

"Children make you want to start life over." ~**Muhammad Ali**

Everyone you meet is going to have an opinion about how you raise your children. You need to have confidence in yourself and do what you think is right. I worked with a girl who was a new mom. One day at lunch, she was talking about having to change her 13 month old son four times the day before because he kept getting dirty. Then she wanted to take a walk but her son was a mess. She was concerned that the neighbors would think she was a slob or a "bad mom". Reality check! Who cares what they think? Kids are supposed to get dirty and messy. That's how they learn. It's O.K. if your house is a mess, too! (to some extent). Do you honestly think you are giving your child the experiences and the quality attention they need by spending your time cleaning your house and worrying about if their clothes are spotless or not? If you are going to church, by all means, clean the kid up. But if you are having a lazy Sunday and you want to take him for a walk while he is still in his pajamas, do it! It could start raining before you get out the door and then you missed the opportunity to spend some quiet time with your child. You have to make the choice. Are you worried about how they look or do you want to spend as much time with your child as you possibly can? It's your choice; but for me it's not even a choice!

Another issue you will encounter as your children grow is hearing people say things Like, "Oh, I could never let my daughter do that." As I've stated, we like to expose our daughters to as many experiences as we can. One of the things we encouraged them to do was embrace any chance they get to travel to see the world and meet new people. Both of our girls received those opportunities while in 5th and 6th grade. Catherine traveled to Mexico and Costa Rica. Audrey went to El Salvador. These were trips arranged through the International School to School

Exchange (I.S.S.E.). Each school sends representatives to the other country with a chaperone. The students live with host families for 3 weeks to immerse themselves in the culture and language. One day I ran into an old acquaintance that has a daughter the same age as Catherine. She asked where CC was. ("CC" is the nickname Catherine decided to use when she entered first grade. On the first day, she told the teacher to call her CC and that is how all of her friends and parents know her. Her parents, on the other hand, have a hard time calling her anything other than Catherine.) I told her she was on an exchange trip in Mexico. This mother gasped, "Oh I could never do that!" Believe me, she wasn't the only person I encountered who had that reaction. My calm response was, "It's not about me." And it wasn't. Sending my children on exchange trips was a way to allow them to see the world and what it has to offer. It allowed them to live with a family for three weeks and improve their Spanish, learn about the Latin American culture, and appreciate what each culture has in common and to embrace the differences. These trips were a great tool for our daughters to mature and learn more about the world. There was nothing in it for me, other than the joy I felt in knowing I was raising cultured and independent daughters. In fact, I was a little jealous of my daughters. They would call and I would be in tears as they told me about their adventures. It was all about them and what they could gain from the experience.

On Catherine's first trip she lived with the family of a famous Mexican soccer player. Her first night there, she sat in the luxury box at his game! What a life! She appreciated it while she was there but she also noted that something was missing from that household. They had a lot of money, several homes in different cities but not much else beside that. The children had a chauffeur to take them places and the parents did their own thing. Catherine noted that there wasn't very much laughter in the household and they didn't really interact together. Catherine returned home a very self assured, responsible ten year old who had developed a sudden love for travel and discovered how to appreciate what she had: not a lot of money but certainly a lot of love and care.

It's amazing to see how each child grows from their unique experiences. Life is an adventure. You just have to be willing to let them go on it. Experiences like these will allow your children to appreciate what they have and the beauty their world has to show them.

French Bread

4 ½ tsp dry yeast

1 ½ tsp salt

1 ½ tsp sugar

2c hot water

5c bread flour

1 egg yolk

1 tbsp water

cornmeal

Mix yeast, sugar and salt with hot water. Let stand 5-10 minutes to ensure activity of yeast. Mix in bread flour. If using stand-mixer, beat 3-5 minutes. Continue kneading on board for 2 minutes. Form a round ball. Place in oiled bowl and cover with plastic wrap for 2 hours or until tripled in bulk. Punch it down and let sit for another hour. Split into 2 sections. Flatten with hands into rectangle about ½" thick. Roll into a loaf. Place on jellyroll pan sprinkled with cornmeal. Repeat with other loaf. Be sure to leave plenty of space between loaves. Cover with slightly damp tea towel for 45 minutes. Heat oven to 400°. Slice top of each loaf a couple of times. Make an egg wash with your egg and brush the top of each loaf. Bake 22-24 minutes. This has a softer crust with a chewy texture. Just the way our family likes it!

Chapter 5
Suggested Musts

"Children must be taught how to think, not what to think." ~ **Margaret Mead**, *cultural anthropologist*

I once knew a woman who decided she was finally going to discipline her boys. The boys were 9 and 10 years old, at the time, and I don't think they had *ever* been disciplined in their short lives. Their mother was actually reading a book called "Have a New Child By Friday. How to Change Your Child's Attitude, Behavior and Character in 5 Days" by Kevin Leman. I had to laugh out loud. Discipline happens from day one! It is not something that can be done quickly. This same woman spent a week's vacation at the beach finding ways NOT to spend time with her children. The root of their discipline problem was lack of attention. Their basic needs of love and attention were not being met so they acted out. She passed up several opportunities to be in the pool playing keep away or out in the ocean, drifting on a raft with them, to go shopping or do other things by herself.

As I go through life, I think back to the things we did with our kids that we are truly grateful for: Playing kickball in the cul-de-sac, taking them to the drive-in even if it was a 45 minute drive to get there, playing bocce ball in the backyard, and roasting marshmallows in the fireplace. Sure, there are a few things we wish we had done different; but generally, we have no regrets. Here is my list of things I think every parent should do with their child(ren):

- **Read to them**
  From the moment you know you are expecting, read to them. Pick up a few children's books and read aloud. You'll be amazed how the baby reacts to your voice in-utero. What you will find is that you

actually start memorizing some of these books. This skill comes in handy when you need to put her down for a nap but no have no book handy and you lack the creativity to make up a story. You can recite one from memory. Trust me, when they are old enough to speak, and you mess up or skip a part, they will let you know!

- **Play with them**
  There will be daily opportunity to entertain and be entertained by your children. Some days you will just want peace and quiet. Other days, you will have the energy to wrestle with them, play kickball or ride bikes. My advice, even on the days you just want peace and quiet, find the energy to play at least one game of "Go Fish" with them. You can set a time limit. When they ask you to play with them, tell them "We can play one game, then mommy needs some quiet time." They will be OK with that and if they aren't, they will learn to be. You are teaching them limits, to respect others and that you do not exist solely to entertain them. It is important for them to know how to play alone as well as how to play with others. But playing with you will be most beneficial overall. They will learn rules but they will also learn how much you love them. Giving your time to them is the most precious thing you can offer your children.

- **Give each child individual attention**
  My friend from the beach needed to realize that the root of her sons' behavior was lack of attention. If she had used the opportunities in their life to spend some one on one time with them, she may have found that they behaved better. It has been my experience that many children act due to a lack of attention from their parents.

- **Take family field trips**
  My husband and I started several traditions with our girls; one of them was a "back to school" dinner". We would let them choose where we would eat dinner the night before school started each summer. The Mellow Mushroom is one of our favorite pizza joints but there isn't any where we live. When we travel, we search them out. We will take a family field trip for one also. We will hop in the car and drive 2 hours, one way, to the closest Mellow Mushroom. The time in the car with the girls, is well worth the drive. Speaking of time in the car -- I once met a Nigerian man at a gas station. We struck up a conversation as we were pumping gas. He was on his way to his son's basketball game and he was not happy with himself. He told me that he was planning to spend some quality alone time with his son in the car on the drive to the game. But he was alone. He said that he got caught up in an issue with the business he

owns and now had to drive alone to the game. I thought this man was wonderful because he was upset that he missed the perfect opportunity to connect with his son. Like me, this man uses the car as an opportunity to check in and reconnect. Instead of riding in silence, or having the kids listen to their i-Pods, they talk to each other. In this fast paced, always electronically connected society, we forget how nice it is to actually sit and talk.

- **Help in their school/attend class field trips**
  This is a great way to show you care and that you are interested in their life. But there is a fine line. Volunteering to help daily is too much. You want to be involved, but not overbearing. John and I used to volunteer once or twice a year to work in the classroom and we would each volunteer to take each girl on one class fieldtrip. That's a great way to get to know their teachers and classmates/friends.

- **Be consistent and follow through**
  Back to my friend at the beach: First of all, if she had been consistent in her discipline from birth, their behavior at ages 9 and 10 wouldn't be a problem. Secondly, there is no fast and easy solution to discipline! It's like dieting. You have to make it a lifestyle change. Third, why on Earth would you put the people around you through that? These are good kids. They just lacked the rules and boundaries that kids need to develop.

- **Set boundaries**
  Kids yearn for boundaries. The rules and boundaries you set let them know that you care. I have even used that to explain to my kids why we will not allow them to do something. You will find that when they are young, they may throw a tantrum over one of your rules but usually they get over it fairly quickly as long as you do not give in! As they get older, they will start questioning your rules. For instance, our girls did not like that we took their cell phones from them at 9:00 each night. They also did not understand why they will have a curfew of midnight when they are older. We used this as an opportunity to have an open dialogue about the rules and boundaries and why we have them.

  We actually asked them why they thought we made these rules. Catherine's initial response was "To torture us." We explained that it was our job as parents to keep them safe, and all of the rules we set up were for their safety. We did not insist that they wear bike helmets because we wanted to embarrass them. It was for their safety. We also took the time to give examples of why this was so important. The bike helmet, for instance, is to prevent head injuries. We told them that their Aunt Beth is a physical therapist and most of the children she works with have head injuries because their parents did not make them wear a helmet. We explained that they are intelligent, beautiful people and we would not want to take the chance of messing that up for them. We told them about how my brother was hit by a car when we were riding our bikes to school one day. Back then, helmets were not a consideration. His leg was broken and he flew into the middle of the street. He was lucky. It could have been much worse. It is a very scary chance you take by not wearing your helmet. While you are young we are responsible for having you follow rules. When you are older, you can choose what rules you want to continue following. Hopefully, you will choose wisely.

The cell phone rule is to help minimize the girl drama (More about that later in this chapter). The curfew is because nothing good ever happens after midnight! Have you ever watched the news? Most of the murders, robberies, rapes, etc. occur after midnight. There is simply no good reason for a child to ever be out after midnight. Period.

You will be amazed at how much information your children retain when you maintain consistent rules and boundaries. Once I was telling the girls about a shooting that occurred and they had to shut down the highway we would take to their school. The first thing Audrey said was "See mom, you were right. Nothing good ever happens after midnight". My heart leapt for joy that she had been listening! Of course, someday there will be a time when she challenges me and stays out past midnight. When that day comes John and I will deal with it – and there will be consequences. But right now, they are satisfied and safe.

- ### Let them learn from you
  One of the best ways to spend time together is when you can teach them something new. Our girls enjoyed learning to cook, so John lets them help in the kitchen. I like to sew and have spent time allowing them to help me or even allow them to make something for themselves. It's great bonding time and creates great memories.

- ### Prepare them for what is coming next
  As adults we forget that we once had to learn how the world works. We assume our kids come equipped with a certain amount of knowledge. But they don't and it is our job to teach them many things. As a parent you have a choice to shelter them from certain events or help them learn from them. If you are choosing to use it as a teachable moment, be sure to present the topic on their level. When the World Trade Center was attacked, CC was in first grade. We were watching the news and felt it was important that she understood what occurred, as much as a seven year old can. We explained that there are bad

people in the world and some bad people had done this. We couldn't tell her why because at the time we really didn't know the reasons behind the attack. This was a great way to reiterate that just because someone is different doesn't make them bad; that we should accept others. It is not our business what another believes in. This allowed her to know what was going on; our explanation was clear and simple but not scary.

A child's life is filled with teachable moments. When you go to a funeral, you can choose to leave them at home or take them with you to experience this part of life and learn from it. We usually chose to take them so they could learn. We would always prepare them for whatever it was we were about to do and what we expected from them. Before a funeral we would explain who the person was and what was going to happen at the funeral. We would tell them that they could talk to the other people there but they could not run around or be loud.

Before vacation we would explain that it would be a long drive and they needed to sleep or play and be patient. This worked great before our first trip to Disney World. They were five and seven and we were going to fly. So our first order of business was to let them know what it would be like to ride in an airplane, since they had never done that before. We explained what behavior was appropriate for an airplane and we even role played being on an airplane. We also told them that this was such a great vacation but it was expensive so they were going to have to try new foods at EPCOT and ride each ride at least once. If they didn't like it after riding it once, they could say so and we would not make them ride it again. But they had to at least try it. This proved to be the best thing we could have ever done. It actually became a habit. Anytime we traveled, they knew they had to try new things. Eventually, they started this practice at home, too.

When Catherine was entering Kindergarten, I tried to prepare her for her first ride on the school bus. I explained that the driver would take care of her. Even though the driver was a stranger, she was allowed to speak to her. Then I told her that the bus would not have seatbelts and that was OK. On her first day, she bravely stepped onto that bus and found a seat. The bus had pulled into our cul-de-sac and came back past me. I was fighting back tears the whole time. I did not want her to see me crying. As she came back past me, she whipped the seatbelt up in the window to show me and very diligently got to work to put it on. The look on her face was, "Look at this mom! How lucky am I to have a seatbelt? And you said there wouldn't be any." I broke down sobbing. I was so happy that she had become so independent, but what she didn't know was that I was sad that she didn't wave as she passed. I had prepared her for what to expect and she was able to adjust when she realized that there were seatbelts in the bus. Since I had taught her the importance of wearing seatbelts, she knew to go ahead and put it on immediately. She did tell me later that none of her subsequent buses had seatbelts.

- **Thank them**

Every chance you get to praise your child, take it. They need to hear it! One of our favorite praises is after some special event or vacation where we really wanted them to be on their best behavior. When we are in the car, leaving an event where they behaved themselves, we tell them how proud we are of them. On the flip side, if they had done something inappropriate during that event, we would point that out as well. Using this system has worked very well for us. It's now very rare that we have to correct them for their behavior at any event. When we do, it is usually because WE failed to properly prepare them for what to expect.

- **Start a tradition of your own**

It is always great to follow your family traditions but it's also really cool to start a tradition of your own. For instance, my paternal grandmother used to cook a big country breakfast of steak, eggs, biscuits and gravy for Christmas morning. When she passed, my dad started cooking the breakfast. Now it is a huge tradition for my brother and I and both of our families. No one wants to miss Christmas breakfast in our household!

John and I are always on the lookout for new traditions. The annual back to school trek to Mellow Mushroom is one. Then we created a New Year's Day tradition. Each New Year's morning John makes Belgian waffles and we serve them topped with our favorite ice cream. Sinful, I know. But utterly delicious! And the girls love this tradition.

- **Parent as a team**

Parenting alone can be a very difficult process. Even single parents need the rest of the village to help, occasionally. John and I may not always agree but we agree more often than not. You need to present a united front. If you allow the kids to play you off of each other, you will certainly find yourself discontented with your spouse and your children. The first time your child asks you if she can spend the night at her friends and you say no, then she goes to ask her dad and he says yes, YOU need to take control. This is another issue with setting consistent boundaries. Explain to her that if she asks one parent, that is the answer. No matter what the topic, one parent is asked and that is the answer. There is no game playing! She may not keep asking until she gets the answer she wants. Then you must follow through and refuse the sleepover. The consequence will fit the crime and it needs to be immediate.

- **Words to live by**

All kids occasionally speak disrespectfully, especially to their own parents. But there are a few people they should always be respectful to: grandparents, police officers, and teachers. Outside of them, your kids will run into people they just don't like and people that really make them angry. One thing we like to tell our girls is to always speak and act respectfully to people. They never know when they will run into them again in their life. They may think that they can tell off some kid in their class, but, that kid may very well be their boss some day. They will have no chance of getting that job if prior interactions with that person were unfavorable. This can be applied to pretty much any person they meet in their life.

Why do I say these are MUST DO's? The thing is, there will be a point in time when your children no longer wish to have you around all the time. So cherish every minute you have with them and make the most of every minute with them so you are sure to instill the values you want them to have.

All of this preparation will come in handy when you are not present. If you have taken the time from the beginning to teach them right from wrong and set boundaries, they will behave wonderfully for other people. Their teachers will praise their behavior. Their friend's parents will praise their behavior. It is always a great boost to your ego and self esteem when another adult tells you how nice and well behaved your children are.

I don't know about you, but that is not something I can lie about. If a kid was unruly while in my care, I politely let their parents know. If they were truly obnoxious, I usually tell my children "they are not welcome back". In my house, there are three golden rules: You must remember your manners, be fairly low maintenance, and be respectful of self, others and personal property. Whenever my children would have a friend over who broke any of these rules, they were usually never asked back.

I would, however, give in from time to time. I remember two friends of Audrey's that were particularly high maintenance. The first was an only child and the entire time she was at our house, she would want to sit and talk to me or have me play with her. She had no idea how to interact with her peers. The other friend was extremely picky about the food we fed her and she never said thank you or cleared her plate. This little girl was in 4th grade and perfectly capable of clearing her plate after dinner. When I took her home, she would get out of my car and never say thank you or goodbye. Over the years, I continued to give her opportunities to correct this behavior that annoyed me so much. Everyone's human. We all make mistakes. We all change. Much to my dismay, this little girl NEVER changed even after many opportunities and prompting from me about what is appropriate. I finally told Audrey that I really didn't care for this friend and was a little surprised when she replied, "I really don't either." It turned out that Audrey had been noticing the rude comments, the lack of manners and high maintenance attitude of this girl and she was choosing not to be her friend. All of my preaching paid off! John and I have always said that we would rather our children misbehave for us and behave when they are not with us. It seems to be working.

Homemade Belgian Waffles

2c flour

2 Tbsp sugar

1 Tbsp baking powder

½ tsp salt

1 ¾ c milk

6 Tbsp oil

2 eggs

Mix all ingredients and let sit for 5 minutes. Using a ¾ c scoop, pour batter into preheated Belgian waffle maker. Cook according to waffle iron instructions. Serve warm topped with your favorite ice cream. We prefer Ben & Jerry's New York Super Fudge Chunk or Graeter's Double Chocolate Chip or Cookies & Cream.

Chapter 6
Character

"Parents can only give good advice or put them on the right paths, but the final forming of a person's character lies in their own hands." ~ **Anne Frank**

Before entering into parenthood, you should know who you are and what your values are. From that, you can work on developing excellent character traits in your children. I'm not saying that your kids will be perfect. Everyone makes mistakes and misjudgments. But you can't expect to have a child who is honest if you yourself are dishonest. Before becoming a parent, you need to take an honest look at yourself. Every little thing you do is magic to your children. They will watch every move you make and parrot it. If there is something in your own character that you don't like, fix it before your children come along.

Parenting is about leading by example. Having a "do as I say, not as I do" attitude will not help you raise children of good character. In fact, not only will their character be poor, but chances are good that your relationship with them will be poor as well. You can't preach to a child not to smoke when you smoke three packs a day. They will soon write you off as a hypocrite. They will even grow to resent you. So live the character you want your children to exhibit.

At this point, some of you may be asking, "What exactly is character? To me, it means having a solid set of values and morals from which to live by. Every family has a slightly different view on character and what's important to them. If you are married, you both need to decide what is most important to your family collectively. John and I agreed that honesty, kindness, and integrity were our top traits. Loyalty is another good one but that comes along later after they have gotten over sibling rivalry and have learned what it really means to be a friend. We'll touch on that later.

One of the benchmarks of good character is treating others the way you want to be treated. This is not an easy concept to teach. I remember trying to get Catherine to understand it. The look on her face was saying, "What on earth are you talking about?" Initially, she thought I was telling her to treat others the way they treat her. I had just scolded her for hitting Audrey. She said, "But mommy, she hit me. You say to treat her the way she treats me." That's when I realized I needed to find a better way of explaining it. I asked her if she would want someone to do that to her. For instance, if she hit her sister again, I would ask, "Do you want someone to hit you when they are not happy with you?" She would tell me, "No". Then I would say, "Then do not hit other people or someday they will hit you." This eventually spread to other concepts such as sharing and respect.

A good time to start discussing rights and responsibilities is around second grade. I have had many people tell me that it is impossible to try to reason with children. I disagree. While they may not "get it" the first time, the more you reinforce it, the more they'll start to understand. Repetition is a great teaching tool. After all, how did you learn your multiplication tables? Keep in mind that strong character doesn't just happen. It develops over time. Every human being has the right to be treated with dignity and respect. We all have a responsibility to treat others with respect which is, interestingly, the way we all expect to be treated.

Chicken & Dumplings

This is a recipe from John's grandmother, Florence Foohey Evard (a.k.a. Flossie). It originally came from the Chicago Tribune in 1901.

3-5 lb hen cut up and covered with water – cook for 1 ½ hrs., with 30 min. left add 1 onion, 2 carrots and 2 chopped celery stalks.

Remove chicken from stock and cool. Debone chicken and place in oval baking dish. Salt and pepper it using the pepper liberally. Strain stock. Reserve 4 cups for sauce. (retain remaining stock for use in other dishes)

2 Tbsp butter and 3 Tbsp flour: make a white roué in a 2 qt saucepan. Add 4 c. stock you had reserved and 1 c milk. Cook until thick. This will take quite a while. Be careful not to burn it. Pour over chicken in baking dish. Top with biscuits (see below). Bake at 350 for 30 minutes.

Biscuit recipe

2 ½ c flour

2 tsp baking powder

1 tsp salt

2 Tbsp butter

1 egg, beaten

milk added to beaten egg to make 8 oz liq.

Mix dry ingredients and cut in butter until butter is pea sized or smaller. Add beaten egg with milk to dough. Do not over mix. Pat out on lightly floured surface to form an oval to fit your baking dish.

Chapter 7
Girl Stuff

Whether you have boys or girls, you are sure to experience the wonderful phenomenon of Relational Aggression (RA). You probably know it as mean girl behavior or bullying. It is a hateful phenomenon. It obliterates a child's self esteem and, rips at your heart. Unless you have experienced it, firsthand, you cannot truly understand it. I have witnessed this behavior through many channels.

Essentially, relational aggression is any form of mean, disrespectful, or bully type behavior. There are victims, bystanders, and aggressors. There are many books you can read to learn more about it and how to handle it, some I have included in the recommended reading section at the end of this book. Some people will claim that the victim must have done something to cause the aggressor to act. I say that is like telling a rape victim that she coerced the rapist! Everyone has been mean at some point in their life. It is part of human behavior. It can be as simple as rolling your eyes at someone else, or turning your back on them as they approach your group. It's usually a covert action. Most girls use the phrase "just kidding" to cover up their behavior. Many times the victim will be a very weak person, one who has trouble standing up for herself or speaking up. But the victim can also be someone who has strong self confidence.

The issue is that the *aggressor* is the one with the problem. The aggressor is usually jealous of the victim for some reason. The aggressor has low self esteem and needs to put someone else down in order to build herself up. As simple as this may sound, it can really impact a child. My daughters will be the first to admit that doing the right thing can be very difficult. But it pays off in the long run.

I recall Catherine crying one day when another girl bullied her at school. We talked about how important it was that she not retaliate and that she always treat others with respect. I remember telling her that, difficult as it was, that she trust me and continue to do the right thing. Frustrated, she yelled, "I'm tired of doing the right thing. It's too hard!" I had to agree. Doing the right thing is never easy. But doing the right thing is important to your well being. Retaliation just perpetuates the cycle of hatred. It is important to move on. The bully will be the person who has the hardest time moving on. She will hold onto things and let them eat her up inside. I refused to allow that to happen to my children. It was important to me that they learn to forgive and move on. I will admit, I remember being mean to some other girls as I was growing up. But I am determined to stop the cycle.

You are probably wondering how on Earth you can protect your child from bullying. Unfortunately, you can't. You can, however, prepare her to deal with it. Here are a few things you can do:

Teach her to always be herself, regardless of what the other kids say. She needs to be a good person and always try to do the right thing. She should not copy their dress style just because the popular girls are doing it. Keep in mind that doing the right thing is usually not easy. Be there for her as she learns these lessons. Remind them to treat others the way they want to be treated. When Catherine was leaving 8th grade, her teachers gave all of the students special awards. Catherine's award was the "True Colors Award" for always being comfortable with herself and consistently showing her "true colors." She finds joy everywhere and shares it with others. We are very proud!

What defines a friend? This is a great discussion question. Your three year- old not be able to answer this, but your seven year old certainly can. They will probably talk about honesty, integrity, openness, etc. The list will look similar to your list of good character traits. Funny how they coincide! Keep in mind that you shouldn't try to get her to be friends with everyone. That's impossible. We are all different and it is human nature to like some people and not like others. We cannot possibly like every person we encounter. We can, however, be respectful to everyone whether we like them or not. An important lesson to learn is that you never know when you will meet someone again in your life. You never want to be disrespectful. It could come back to haunt you.

Tell her why girls act this way and let her read some of the books at the end of this book. Girls who behave this way have low self esteem. They have to put someone else down in order to build themselves up. Tell her that sometimes they are jealous of what you have or how you look or even how you handle yourself in any given situation. Maybe you are a confident young lady. Mean girls lack that confidence and they will do what they can to bring you down to their level.

Most of all, encourage her to always do the right thing and continue to be herself. It will be difficult and sometimes painful. But it will be worth it and she will grow to be a strong respectful woman.

Soft Pretzels

2 C Hot water	1 egg
4 ½ tsp dry yeast	6-7 c flour
½ c sugar	1 egg yolk
2 tsp salt	2 Tbsp water
¼ c softened butter	sea salt

Dissolve yeast in water, add salt, sugar, butter, egg and about 3 c flour. Mix well with dough hook by hand. Add about 2 more cups of flour. Beat with dough hook by hand until incorporated. Add last cup of flour. Beat with dough hook on the stand mixer. Check to see if any more flour is needed. Dough should be stiff.

Remove dough and knead into ball. Place in oiled bowl and cover with plastic wrap. Refrigerate 3-5 hours or over night.

When ready to make them, tear dough into small pieces and form into 3 inch sticks. Place sticks on cookie sheet. Cover full try with tea towel and let rise 20 minutes. Uncover nad brush with egg wash. Sprinkle with sea salt.

Bake at 400 for 15 minutes.

Cool slightly before serving with melted cream cheese to dip in.

These pretzels freeze well. If you have leftovers, simply reheat for 10 minutes at 350.

Chapter 8
You Have To Let Them Fail... To A Degree

"Life is finite. Live it fully with no regrets. Embrace change because it's someplace you've never been before."
~ **Richard Simmons**

"You have to let them fail" is something my mother-in-law says often. I'm not saying I disagree but it's a gray area. Here are a couple of stories:

On the first day of first grade for Audrey, she came home upset. She had met a new friend but the little girl sitting behind her said, "Don't talk to her--she's black." Audrey retorted with, "So--she's my friend." Audrey and the "black girl" have been best buds ever since, even after they each changed schools. Those types of things make you feel great as a parent and they remind you that all of your preaching is sinking in.

When Catherine was entering 8th grade, she ran for student council president. (She was running against another girl and a boy.) On election day, Catherine lost to her male classmate by only three votes. One of her teachers came to me and told me how close the tally was. She knew how disappointed Catherine was and she wanted me to know that it wasn't a landslide. She also wanted me to know how highly she and many of the other faculty members thought of Catherine. She didn't have to tell me any of this but she chose to. She told me because she thought my daughter was a strong and decent person. Again, I felt great about how we have raised our girls. Truthfully, I held a private grudge against "Mr. President" throughout the first quarter of the school year. Then I came to my senses. As badly as Catherine wanted the title, she didn't need it to continue leading her classmates and being a great person.

It is important for children to have disappointments or make mistakes and to learn from them. Of course, there are some times when you need to step in before they make that mistake. For instance, when it comes to sex and drugs, you do not want them to "try it out" and make a mistake that they will regret for the rest of their lives. So talk to them when they are young about the dangers and responsibilities of each. If you teach them about right and wrong, it will be up to them to make the right choices. Other things, like getting a poor grade on a test because they chose not to study, are good teaching lessons. You will lecture and preach until you're blue in the face and they will not listen to you about their study habits. Sometimes you have to let them fail so they can figure out their mistakes then they will work ten times harder to get their grade back to what you have discussed is acceptable. Keep in mind that every child is not a genius and that for some, a "C" is the best they can do. Some kids struggle with school as a whole or just in one subject. That is for your family to work out. My point is that there are times they will not listen to you and you will have to let them learn from their mistakes. But when we are talking about morals and character, you need to do all of your work upfront and hope and pray that they make good choices when left to their own devices. My husband and I always say we would rather they act up for us at home versus acting up for others when we are not there. It's always great when other people, tell you how great your children are. Trust me… people will not say you have great kids unless they mean it.

Dad's Pizza

This dough recipe is a work in progress. We usually have pizza every Friday night. Sometimes we order out but usually John makes it from scratch. Every time he makes it, he finds some way to improve it. The dough can also be rolled into individual servings for calzones.

2 ¼ tsp yeast

1c warm water

1c all-purpose flour

½ tsp salt

1 tbsp olive oil

1 tbsp honey

1 ½-2c bread flour

pizza cheese

Your favorite toppings

egg wash made with one yolk

Mix yeast, warm water, and all-purpose flour in a stand mixer on low until smooth. Add salt, olive oil and honey. Add bread flour as needed until the dough comes together no longer sticks to the bottom of the bowl. Attach the dough hook and knead for 10 minutes. Add more bread flour as needed to stop dough from sticking to bowl. Remove from mixing bowl and place in large oiled ceramic bowl. Cover with plastic wrap and let rise for 1 hour. Punch it down then let rise for another 1-2 hours until almost doubled in size. Split in half. Roll to about ¼" thickness on floured surface. If using for pizza, let rolled out dough rise (covered) for 20 minutes. Using a fork, poke holes all over the dough to prevent bubbles in baking. Spread your favorite tomato or pizza sauce on the dough. Brush edge of crust with egg yolk. Sprinkle your toppings and cheese. Bake at 450 for 10-12 minutes.

Chapter 9
Experience and Exposure

"Nothing is a waste of time if you use the experience wisely." ~**Auguste Rodin**

Experience and exposure is a pairing I talk about repeatedly. They go together like bacon and eggs, or Oreos and milk. You can't have one without the other! Exposing your children to different things and creating unique experiences for them provides them with a great amount of learning. You see, learning doesn't occur just in the classroom. It's up to parents to provide learning experiences throughout their life. When your children are young, you can start by teaching them the ABC song when you are pushing them on the swing. They can learn to count by picking up rocks (or any "treasure") when you take a walk. We take a yearly trip to the antique mall with grandma and grandpa. You'd be amazed what they can learn there! Did you know that most kids in 2009 have never seen a phonograph? Some of them are unaware what an LP is. They only know of CD's and iTunes. Things like these help give them a little history lesson as well as perspective about the evolution from phonograph to i-pod!

Too often I meet people who never travel outside of their city. There is a world to experience out there and it doesn't have to be expensive. (A trip to Washington D.C. is probably the cheapest vacation you can imagine. Most everything you do there is free!) Travel provides you and your children with the opportunity to see firsthand that most people in this world live much like we do. Travel can provide insight and understanding into other cultures which broadens the young mind. Travel also can help make connections between what your children learn in a book and what they see in real life. When my girls travel, they usually tell me things like, "The rainforest is really humid and you are soaking when you come out of it, even though it's not really raining in there." Plus, it's one thing to read about the Grand Canyon. It's another thing to actually see it! For example, since we live in the Midwest, we don't really get to see spectacular sunrises or sunsets. So when we take a trip to an ocean area, we make sure the girls witness the beauty of the beginning or ending of the day. One of our favorite trips is to Disney's Epcot Center. We spend the whole day experiencing the different cultures and eating food that is unique to many parts of the world.

There is so much for them to learn and we can choose to leave it all to their teachers or we can have a hand in it too. As your children approach high school and college, they are going to talk about jobs and careers. Do yourself and your child a favor and don't wait until they are a senior in high school to think about any of it. All of their life experiences can help mold their choices for the future. The more experiences they have and the more things they are exposed to, the more information they have to help themselves make choices. If they only know the job mom does, then that will be all they think about. But truly, they may not be interested in it or even understand what is really involved.

<u>Jambalaya</u>

John and I have made this dish together since before we were married. It is proof that if you continue to put foods on your children's plates, they will eventually eat it. At first the girls would not touch it. But the more we cooked it and ate it in front of them, the more curious they became. In no time at all, they were begging us to make it for them.

5 lbs chicken breasts

4 tbsp butter

1 ½ c chopped onions

1 ½ c chopped green pepper

1 ½ c chopped celery

1 tbsp Tabasco sauce

½ lb tasso cubed

If using tasso, this dish will be very spicy. You may wish to use regular ham and have a creole sauce on the side for those who which to add a little spice to their meal.

¾ c tomato sauce

2c uncooked rice

3 c chicken stock

Seasoning mix

2 bay leaves

1 tsp salt

1 tsp each of white pepper, black pepper, red pepper

1 tsp garlic powder

Make a stock: Remove skin and cut meat from chicken bones. Refrigerate meat. Put bones in stock pot and cover with about 4 cups water. Cook on high 20 minutes. Simmer for one hour and skim foam occasionally. Then strain the stock and use in the recipe.

Melt butter in 4qt heavy pot. Add ½ of the onions, peppers and celery into pot with tasso, spice mix and Tabasco. Cook on medium for 20 minutes stirring constantly. Add remaining onions, peppers and celery. Cook 5 minutes, stirring frequently. Add tomato sauce, simmer 5 minutes, stirring constantly. Add chicken, stir occasionally for 15 minutes. Stir in rice. Reduce heat and cook for 12 minutes. Add stock you recently made. Bring to boil, reduce heat, cover and cook 15 minutes. Serve warm with French bread.

Chapter 10
Take A Break

"Lust is easy. Love is hard. Like is most important." ~ **Carl Reiner**

When you need a break, do you go out for ladies night? Do you and your spouse take a vacation together? Do you and the family do something special?

There is no right or wrong answer. You just have to be happy with your choices.

It was my preference to travel with my husband AND children when they were little. As they grew older, I didn't feel guilty about leaving them while I had some down time. I have the best time when I can see my girls' faces light up when they experience something new or see the beautiful sunrise at Virginia Beach for the first time. (They spontaneously hugged each other at the sight of the sunrise. Honest! This was not a staged photo. One of my fondest memories though!)

Plus I enjoyed the opportunities to make memories and really get to know each other while we were together. My girls will be adults all too soon. John and I will have to travel without them eventually. On the other hand, we have friends that travel yearly without their children. We have other married friends who travel with their friends a regular basis. Everyone needs a mental vacation. Do what works for you.

Outside of vacation, it's important for you and your spouse to have alone time as well. Since John and I choose to travel with the kids, it's imperative that we get the occasional date night. Some couples like to set up a monthly or even weekly date. We are more sporadic, but any way you do it is fine. Just make sure you do it!

You choose how often and what you do based on your interests and financial status. Once the girls started babysitting, one of the neighbors told me "We need to go out alone occasionally to remind us that we still like each other." Sometimes John and I just take a walk. Other times we go out for dinner or a movie. Lately, we have found complete joy by going to the grocery store together on Sunday mornings. Our local Kroger has a Starbucks in it. I get my caramel macchiato with extra whip, John gets his double shot espresso and we gather a few groceries. Peacefully, we meander the aisles and laugh about this being our new favorite way to date. We joke about how we will do it when we retire to a warmer climate. It's fun and relaxing. And who knows—you may find the person who gave you butterflies many years ago when you first started dating.

Hot Chocolate and Toast (A winter favorite)

This is totally a comfort food. But is something the girls and I like to eat together, especially after we've been playing out in the snow.

Make your favorite hot chocolate.

Be sure to add the gourmet toppings like whipped cream, marshmallows and caramel drizzle.

Make some buttered toast. 3 pieces each should do.

Dip your toast into the hot chocolate and eat it. Delicious!

Chapter 11
In a Nutshell

"Children are unpredictable. You never know what inconsistency they're going to catch you in next."
~Franklin P. Jones

If you get nothing else out of this book, I hope you at least walk away with a list of things you might like to do with your family. I have learned that the more I hear something, the better I learn it. The same goes for kids. Repetition is a great teacher. Repeat yourself throughout their childhood. They will thank you for it. Sometimes they will make fun of you for it, but they will learn and be grateful that you taught them some valuable morals and character traits.

In a nutshell:

1. Date your children – Take them out for an ice cream or dinner. Make time to spend time alone with each of them. This allows you to get to know each of them as individuals and it helps cut down on sibling rivalry.
2. Don't worry about what other people think; do what is right for your family and be confident in that choice.
3. Never put off hugging your child or telling them that you love them.
4. Let them have a special item. My girls each have an "animal blanket". It's basically a security blanket. I had a stuffed Winnie the Pooh when I was growing up. I still have him but he is hidden in a Rubbermaid container in my basement. Each of my girls has a special box like this, too. They keep things that are meaningful to them but they have outgrown. It may be a doll or an item of clothing. The one thing they

hold onto nightly is their animal blanket. Audrey's doesn't even have animals on it but that is what they call them. Thread bare, smelly but loved…well loved. Both of them are to the point where they leave it home when they sleepover a friend's house. It is something to hold onto. There is nothing wrong with that. I have John in bed with me every night. Why should they be alone?

5. Laugh with them daily. Laughter makes everything better.
6. Document what they say. I started jotting down the funny things they would say in a scrapbook. At 3 years of age, Catherine helped John out when he was driving. Someone in front of John was not driving to John's liking. He started yelling at the man. John said, "Drive!" and Catherine followed that up with, "Asshole!"

   At age 2, Audrey shouted "I need a fu**ing spoon". After a brief investigation I discovered that what she was really saying was "I need a fork and spoon." Both are funny…now. But at the time John and I had to get a handle on our language. (I guess #6A would be "Be careful what you say)
7. Be there. Mentally and physically. Sometimes they need advice. Sometimes they just need a hug. Know what they need when they need it and stop whatever else you are doing when your children need you. Keep in mind that they hold you in high regard, especially when they are young. I once had a teacher who said that kids are like a bucket of water. Each phrase you speak and each action you perform either adds water to the bucket or takes water out of the bucket. The goal is to fill your child's bucket. (Stabile, 2004) You alone will destroy your relationship with your children. Think before you act and speak. Be there for them in all ways.
8. Set boundaries. This goes for dating, cell phones, television, bedtime, curfew, etc. You set boundaries because you care; not because you want to torture them. Children need boundaries to feel secure. It helped them feel loved and your children will grow to appreciate the boundaries and you.
9. Teach them. Every day is filled with teachable moments. Don't let them pass you by no matter how many times your children complain. Teach them to laugh at themselves, to be confident, to be responsible, and to appreciate others for who they are. Teach them to accept others. Teach them to budget their time and money. Teach them what to expect and have expectations of them.
10. Enjoy your children… enough said.

Pasta Audrey

One day, the girls decided they were going to make dinner. First they made homemade chicken noodle soup. They actually videotaped it as if they were making a cooking show. Then Audrey made this meal.

8 oz rigatoni, uncooked

1/4c grated Parmesan cheese

8 slices bacon in 1" pieces

pinch of cayenne pepper

2c. broccollini flowerets

mozzarella cheese, shredded

1½ tsp minced garlic

Cook rigatoni according to package directions; drain. Be careful not to overcook. In large skillet, cook bacon over medium high heat, stirring frequently about 7 minutes (until bacon is browned). Reduce to medium heat. Add broccoli and garlic. Cook, stirring occasionally until broccoli is al dente (about 3 minutes). Add rigatoni and remaining ingredients, except the basil and cheese. Put generous helpings into individual, oven safe, serving bowls. Top generously with mozzarella and bake at 350 for about 4 minutes to melt cheese. Yummy!

Chapter 12
The Future

Do what you feel in your heart to be right- for you'll be criticized anyway. You'll be damned if you do, and damned if you don't. **~Eleanor Roosevelt**

Always remember that you have much to be thankful for! Make a list of all of the things you and your family are thankful for.   It is a great bonding experience and, if you have teenagers, a reality check. Teens tend to be very self-centered. Get them involved in community service early and have them help create this list. You will see a difference in your children. You'll also have a proud moment when you hear all of the things they want to add to the list.

Fair Warning…

Your children will:

- Pick on you
- Puke in your car
- Disregard your rules
- Repeat your words--usually at the most inopportune time
- Love you, unconditionally. You should do the same with them.

It's how you deal with these little things that will mold your children as people of character.

The best way to alienate your children is to make a big deal over any of the above. You will also alienate them if you pick on them, compare them in a negative way to their siblings or friends; neglect to praise them; change the rules arbitrarily; are ungrateful; or yell at them because they did not understand what you said without first rephrasing what you say. Whatever you do, make sure you follow your own rules. It will strengthen your relationship with yourself and your kids.

This is especially important as children become teens. You will expect more from them in terms of responsibility and maturity as they begin babysitting, using cell phones, driving, and dating. Before they reach these milestones, they will be watching you, very closely. They will question why they cannot text and drive if they see you do it. So think ahead about the rules you will be enforcing with them. Then start following your own rules immediately.

When they enter school, make sure they are armed with self respect and a sense of responsibility. This will pay off in the long run. The sooner they understand their role in their future, the more responsible they will be.

Your future as an empty nester?

You know… I was never one of those parents who shooed my kids off to school at the end of summer or cheered as they rode off on the bus. Every first day of school was emotional for me. I wanted summer to last forever. Those carefree days are few and far between the older they get. I try to make the most out of every summer with them. As my children approach adulthood, I am proud of what we have raised and I am glad my children are independent, responsible people. But it's hard to let them go and think about life without them in our daily lives. As hard as it is, I know I need to consider what we will do with ourselves when the girls are grown. This is another one of those events I need to mentally prepare for. I know I have preached about mentally preparing for certain life events. The only way for me to revert back into being a wife again and not the mother in a family of 4 was to really start mentally preparing myself WAY ahead of time. I think I was 35 when we started kicking around the different ideas of what we would do once the kids were grown. At 40 I knew it was closer than I wanted it to be. When my eldest proudly reported that she "would be going to college in just 5 short years," I almost wrecked my car! That was a major sign to me that I really needed to take my own advice seriously.

While we haven't figured out exactly HOW we are going to do it, John and I have had many conversations about WHAT we want to do. The WHEN is still iffy, too. But we do know it will be in the next 10-15 years. It's never too early to start planning! We have always had a dream of opening a Bed & Breakfast, but that has morphed into a café in a warmer climate. We both love what we do and have considered moving south and continuing our careers. It's up in the air. The important thing is we are brainstorming and making plans and we have dreams and some goals. All I can do is offer up a little advice:

1. **Train your children to keep in touch with you and each other.**

   It is very easy to move across town and not speak to your family. Sometimes we think that is what we want. But you will be very lonely later in life if you allow your children to slip away like that. I know we raised them to be independent. But we have also raised them to be respectful and caring. If you have done your job right, your children will want to keep in touch with you; no matter where they live in this world.

   However, that doesn't just happen. I learned the hard way that this was one of those things that needed to be spelled out for them. As I mentioned earlier in the book, we have sent our children on many trips. Each trip has contributed to their development as an independent, responsible person. When Catherine was on her 8th grade trip to Washington D. C., a chaperone notified all of the parents that they had all had arrived safely. I was cool with that. The next day I wanted to actually speak to my daughter so I left her a message. No response. I texted her asking how the sites were that day. Her response: "Good." I asked another quick question and got yet another one word answer! So I continued with another question and was quickly answered with "I'll tell you when I get home." So I replied with "When you are away you are expected to speak to your parents. Even when you are 40 years old you are expected to call and tell us that you have arrived safely to where ever you are going and you are to keep us informed with more than one word answers." Catherine replied "o.k."…. then she actually called later and told me about her day. That was all I was asking for. I was not trying to be intrusive and I certainly knew she was safe. The point was that she needed to remember where she came from and stay connected. It is my job to raise her but it is her job to be thankful for all she has been given and respectful to those who gave it to her.

   Siblings can sometimes be the worst at staying connected. We have tried to train the girls to tell each other how much they love each other. We have also tried to help them develop a relationship that wants to stay together. Many times siblings marry into other families and end up in completely different worlds even though they still live in the same city. We don't want our girls to be like that. So we have made an effort to see or call our siblings as often as we can. We have also told our children that we expect them to call each other every other day when they are away. Hopefully, when they are in college, they will make it a point to call and talk to each other. Then it will be a habit when they are married. Sibling rivalry does not have to last all their life.

   We love both of our girls equally but differently. They are completely different people and we love both of them for who they are. Eventually they should catch on to that. They seem to have a very good relationship with each other. Cell phones and e-mail have really helped build relationships. Some may say they are the worst thing to happen to a family but I think they are great. We set limits on when they can use them but also told them that we EXPECT them to use technology to stay in touch with us and each other.

For instance, a couple of our rules are: no cell phones at the dinner table or while we are having a conversation; no cell phone usage after 9pm (until they hit high school, then we extended it to 10pm); no cell phones while they are visiting with family, etc. However, if one of them is out of town, it is ok for them to use their phone anytime to stay connected to the rest of the family. By the way, these rules are a work in progress. Remember, we learn from our mistakes and I do not hesitate to change the rules if I've found one to be a mistake. It's been hard, but I have learned to admit my mistakes.

2. **Faith, Hope and Love**
   Have faith that you have raised them well.

   Hope that they make good choices for themselves and for your family.

   Love them no matter what. Because that is what parenting is all about.

Cinnamon Rolls

These are the most deliciously sinful rolls you will ever taste. Beware: Your children will request that you serve them for breakfast when they have friends sleepover.

1 c heavy cream

1 ½ c flour

4 tsp baking powder

½ tsp salt

2 TBSP melted butter

2 TBSP gr. cinnamon

1/2c light brown sugar, packed

Topping:

1/2c light brown sugar, packed

2 TBSP heavy cream

1 tsp vanilla

Preheat oven to 425.

In a mixer bowl, whip the cream until stiff. In a small bowl, whisk together the flour, baking powder, and salt. Add to the whipping cream gradually stirring gently until a dough is formed. Transfer to a lightly floured surface and knead for 1 minute. Roll the dough into a rectangle (about 10x13). Spread the melted butter over the dough and sprinkle with the cinnamon and brown sugar.

Start at the long side and roll into a jelly roll. Using a serated knife, cut into slices about ½" thick or so. Place rolls close together in a greased 12x7 pan and bake for 15 minutes or until the top of the rolls is golden.

Prepare the topping in a small bowl. Remove rolls from oven and spread the topping mixture over each roll. Return to oven for 3-4 minutes or until topping starts to bubble. Serve warm.

Works Cited

Brett, Regina. "Regina Brett's 45 life lessons and 5 to grow on". *blog.cleveland.com*. Updated: Wednesday, October 28, 2009, 9:49 AM. Web. Accessed July 21, 2012. http://blog.cleveland.com/pdextra/2007/09/regina_bretts_45_life_lessons.html.

Kushner, Harold S. *When Bad Things Happen to Good People*. New York: Schocken, 1981. Print.

Myra, Harold Lawrence, and Jane Kurisu. *Santa, Are You for Real?* Nashville: Tommy Nelson, 1997. Print.

Stabile, Michael J. *H.E.L.P. Healthy Effective Lessons In Parenting*. Cincinnati: FutureNow Consulting, LLC, 2004. Print.

Recommended reading

1. Dellasega, Cheryl, and Charisse Nixon. *Girl Wars: 12 Strategies That Will End Female Bullying*. New York: Simon & Schuster, 2003. Print.
2. Several of the American Girl books

The future belongs to those who believe in their beauty of their dreams.~ Eleanor Roosevelt

Printed in the United States
By Bookmasters